GREAT RIVERS

The RHINE

Michael Pollard

Evans

Evans Brothers Limited

First published in 1997 by Evans Brothers Limited

Evans Brothers Limited
2a Portman Mansions
Chiltern Street
London W1U 6NR

© Evans Brothers Limited 1997
First published in paperback in 2002

Commissioned by: Su Swallow
Consultant: Stephen Watts
Design: Neil Sayer
Editor: Debbie Fox
Picture research: Victoria Brooker
Maps: Hardlines

British Library Cataloguing in Publication Data.

Pollard, Michael, 1931
    The Rhine. – (Great Rivers)
    1. Rhine River – Juvenile literature 2. Rhine River Valley
    Juvenile literature
    I. Title
    943.4

    ISBN 0 237 52435 X

Printed in Hong Kong by Wing King Tong

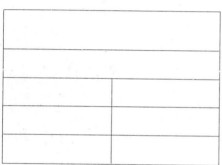

ACKNOWLEDGEMENTS

For permission to reproduce copyright material, the author
and publishers gratefully acknowledge the following:

Cover (main image) Freek van Arkel/Hollandse Hootgte (bottom left) Colin Varndell/Bruce Coleman Ltd (bottom right) Atlantide/Bruce Coleman Ltd
Title page Robert Harding Picture Library
page 8 Tony Stone **page 9** Geospace/SPL **page 10** Woodfall Wild Images/D. Woodfall **page 11** Bruce Coleman/Massimo Borchi **page 12** Travel Ink/Andrew Cowin **page 13** AKG **page 15** (top) Popperfoto/Reuter (bottom) Popperfoto **page 16** (top) AKG (bottom) Travel Ink/Andrew Cowin **page 17** Robert Harding Picture Library **page 18** Magnum/Fred Mayer **page 19** (top) Tony Stone (bottom) Image Bank **page 20** Tony Stone **page 21** (top) Tony Stone (bottom) Bruce Coleman/Dr Eckart Pott **page 22** Bruce Coleman/Atlantide **page 23** (top) Hugh McKnight (bottom) Bruce Coleman/Hans-Peter Merten **page 24** (left) CNES, 1994 Destribution Spot Image/Science Photo Library (right) Zefa **page 25** Zefa **page 27** AKG **page 28** Robert Harding Picture Library **page 29** Hugh McKnight **page 30** Zefa **page 31** (top) Jurgen Drenth/Hollandse Hoogte (bottom left) Bruce Coleman/Paul van Gaalen (bottom right) Magnum/Fred Mayer **page 32** Freek van Arkel/Hollandse Hoogte **page 33** Dries Hondebrink/Hollandse Hoogte **page 34** Das Fotoarchiv **page 35** (top) Tony Stone (bottom) Stephanie Colasanti **page 36** (bottom) Bruce Coleman/Colin Varndell (top) Bruce Coleman/Andy Purcell **page 37** Tony Stone **page 38** Travel Ink/Andrew Cowin **page 39** (top) Zefa (bottom) Bruce Coleman/Hans Reinhard **page 40** (top) AKG (bottom) Das Fotoarchiv/Thomas Mayer **page 41** Das Fotoarchiv **page 42 (top)** The International Commission for the Protection of the Rhine (bottom) BASF **page 43** (left) Stephanie Colantsi (right) Robert Harding Picture Library

CONTENTS

A KEY WATERWAY

THE RHINE IS ONE OF EUROPE'S MAJOR RIVERS. IT IS NOT EUROPE'S LONGEST, BUT IT IS THE BUSIEST. MANY CITIES ON ITS BANKS ARE MAJOR PORTS OR CENTRES OF INDUSTRY.

THE RHINE STARTS ITS JOURNEY to the North Sea as two streams high in the glaciers and mountains of the Swiss Alps. The Hinterrhein flows from the Rheinwaldhorn glacier, which is over 2200 metres high in the mountains. Then it meets the Vorderrhein, which springs from Lake Toma, 150 metres higher. The combined streams, or tributaries, are joined by others, which all flow between Austria and the tiny state of Liechtenstein and then northwards into Lake Constance.

After running west between Germany and Switzerland to Basle, the Rhine turns north and for about 200 kilometres forms the national boundary between Germany and France. The river flows on through north-western Germany and then through the Netherlands to reach the North Sea.

A WORKING RIVER

For thousands of years the Rhine has been a transport route for the people who live near it. Today, it is used by ocean-going ships from its mouth in the North Sea to Cologne in Germany, and barges carry cargoes as far as Basle in Switzerland. The Rhine is really the spine of a network of navigable rivers and canals, and it is part of a waterway linking the North Sea with the Black Sea.

THE RHINE IN HISTORY

The width of the Rhine, at one time up to four kilometres in places, made it a natural boundary between

▶ Steeply shelving hillsides enclose the Rhine as it flows northwards through Germany. Katz Castle was one of the famous fortresses and watchtowers built by German noble families.

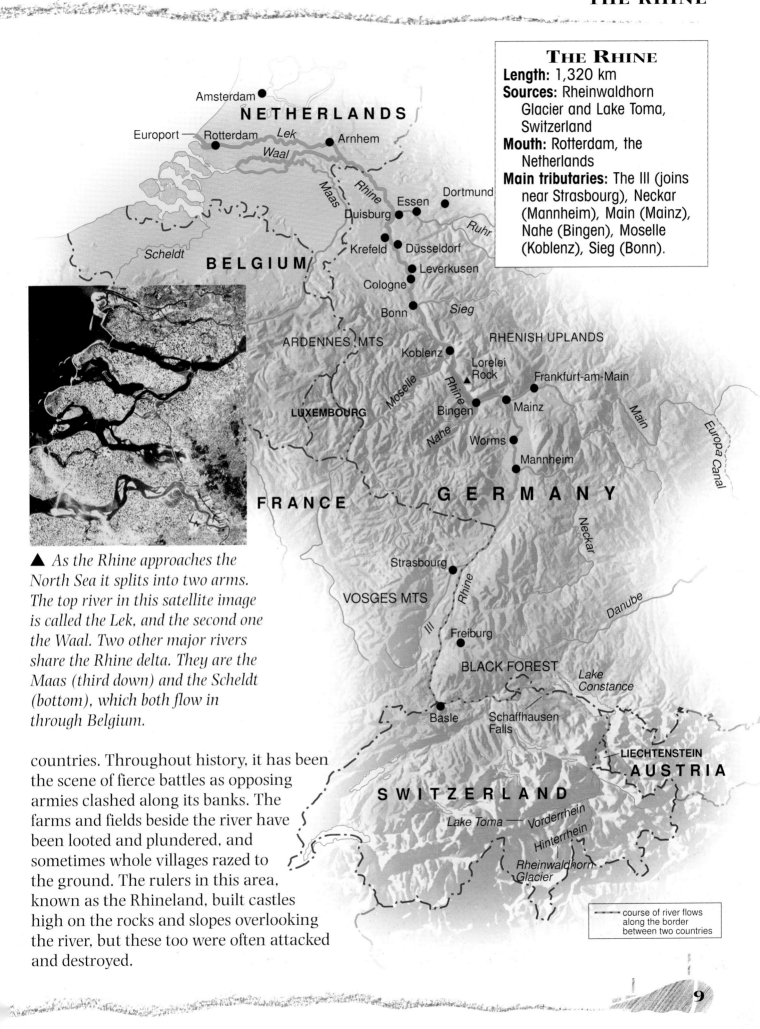

THE RHINE
Length: 1,320 km
Sources: Rheinwaldhorn Glacier and Lake Toma, Switzerland
Mouth: Rotterdam, the Netherlands
Main tributaries: The Ill (joins near Strasbourg), Neckar (Mannheim), Main (Mainz), Nahe (Bingen), Moselle (Koblenz), Sieg (Bonn).

▲ As the Rhine approaches the North Sea it splits into two arms. The top river in this satellite image is called the Lek, and the second one the Waal. Two other major rivers share the Rhine delta. They are the Maas (third down) and the Scheldt (bottom), which both flow in through Belgium.

countries. Throughout history, it has been the scene of fierce battles as opposing armies clashed along its banks. The farms and fields beside the river have been looted and plundered, and sometimes whole villages razed to the ground. The rulers in this area, known as the Rhineland, built castles high on the rocks and slopes overlooking the river, but these too were often attacked and destroyed.

course of river flows along the border between two countries

HOW THE RHINE WAS FORMED

OVER MILLIONS OF YEARS, THE EARTH'S OUTER LAYER, OR CRUST,
WENT THROUGH MANY CHANGES BEFORE THE EARTH TOOK
ON ITS PRESENT-DAY SHAPE.

ABOUT 100 MILLION YEARS AGO, separate pieces, or plates, of the Earth's crust moved and collided, producing huge upward folds. These folds were made up of rocks that had been formed beneath the sea and were brought to the surface by the pressure of the plates pushing sideways on them. The folds became the world's great mountain ranges, such as the Alps in Europe and the Himalayas in southern Asia.

▼ *Glaciers like this one, high in the Swiss Alps, once covered the whole of northern Europe, scouring out river courses as they moved slowly towards the sea.*

THE GREAT ICE AGE

About one million years ago, vast sheets of ice up to 3000 metres thick began to cover North America and northern Europe, including the Alps. This was the Ice Age. At that time, all the waters of the Alps flowed to the south. These huge ice-sheets had two effects on the Earth's surface. First, their great weight made it sink in some places by as much as 900 metres. Second, they formed glaciers, which are moving streams of ice and snow. As the glaciers moved, usually at the rate of about one metre a day over hundreds of years, they scoured out new channels on

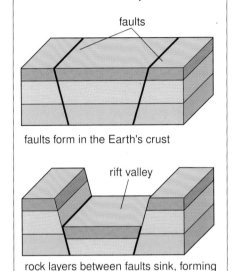

RIFT VALLEYS

Faults are cracks in the Earth's crust. When there are two faults side by side, the rocks between them sometimes sink. This forms a steep-sided, flat-bottomed valley. Geologists call this a rift valley.

faults

faults form in the Earth's crust

rift valley

rock layers between faults sink, forming a rift valley

▲ *The Rhine cuts its way through the wooded hills of northern Germany near Marksburg.*

the surface. By about 10,000 years ago the world's climate was warming up and the ice was melting fast. When glaciers slid across the landscape, they formed new valleys and left scattered rocks and screes – layers of smaller stones – behind them. The sides of some valleys were so steep that they collapsed in landslides, blocking the valley floors and creating lakes. The only way the water could escape was by cutting deep gorges through the debris.

A NEW COURSE

In the Alps the route of the streams to the south was now blocked by these landslides. The water had to find a new way out of the mountains. It drained into a hollow which became Lake Constance. When the hollow was full the water had to escape, so it forced its way through limestone cliffs to form the Schaffhausen Falls. Continuing westwards round the mountains of the Black Forest, the river turned north trying to find a way through to a lower level. It entered a steep-sided rift valley about 32 kilometres wide, formed when the Earth's crust was cooling and settling. Moving north, the river found another range of mountains in its way. It was held up there until the water level had risen enough for the water to push its way through the slate rocks. Even today, it is possible to see rocks marked with old water levels. From then on, the Rhine could flow easily. Ahead, as far as the North Sea, was the North German Plain. This area lay for thousands of years under huge sheets of ice several hundred metres deep. The land sank under their weight. When the glacier moved, it levelled everything in its path. For the last 200 kilometres of its journey, the Rhine became increasingly sluggish as it crossed this flat, low-lying land. Finally, it broke up into broad channels as it moved through the Netherlands to the North Sea.

SETTLERS ON THE RHINE

THE FIRST PEOPLE TO SETTLE ALONG THE RHINE VALLEY CAME FROM THE EAST IN ABOUT 5000 BC.

IN THE FERTILE SOIL THE SETTLERS GREW WHEAT, barley, rye, peas and beans. The wooded hillsides provided timber for the frames of their houses and foraging for their pigs. Every year, as the snows of the Alps melted, the fields were flooded. Some of the land remained swampy all year round and outbreaks of fever would sweep through the settlements. There were dangers from outside too. New settlers from eastern Europe, fleeing from invaders in their own land, sometimes attacked the Rhine villages. The villagers who were driven out moved on and built new settlements. By about 800 BC the people of the Rhine had created a distinct civilisation, which is called the Celtic culture. Round about 200 BC, tribes from northern Europe also began to move into the valley.

WHEN THE ROMANS CAME

Under Julius Caesar, the Romans built up an empire that stretched across western Europe as far as the Rhine. Roman troops first set up camp along the river in 56 BC and stayed for 500 years. The Romans accepted the Rhine as the border of their empire, but attacks from the eastern side drove them to retaliate. Caesar's soldiers built a bridge at Neuwied, just north of Koblenz, but it was soon destroyed by the flow of the river. Each time the Romans marched east, they were forced to retreat. They built forts to watch over the eastern bank and a fleet of armed boats to patrol the river. The upper river was easier to cross, and the Romans set up camp on the eastern side. But attacks from hostile tribes continued. In AD 83 work began on a line of forts, linked by earth and stone walls, which ran for about 60 kilometres parallel to the eastern bank before veering away to the east. This wall, the *Limes Germanicus*, helped to keep out attackers, but it did not stop them completely.

◀ *The remains of a Roman fort on the* Limes Germanicus. *The line of forts is absolutely straight for more than 80 kilometres of its length.*

▲ *The Huns' invasion of western Europe in* AD *451, led by Attila. They left a trail of terror behind them, destroying villages and looting livestock.*

THE HUNS ATTACK

In AD 451 a powerful army of Huns, behind their leader Attila, set out from their base in Hungary to conquer western Europe. There were 70,000 Hun soldiers, many of them skilled horsemen and all ferocious fighters. Attila marched on across the Rhine and into France. Near Troyes, in north-eastern France, the Huns and the Romans met. The battle raged all day, and the slaughter of men and horses was terrible. Finally the Huns were forced to retreat behind the barrier of the Rhine and return home. The Huns did not make another attempt to conquer western Europe, but the Roman empire, too, was in its last days. Before long, the Roman troops left for home.

EARLY SETTLERS AND INVADERS

BC
c.5000: Peoples from the Balkans in south-east Europe moved westward and settled along the Rhine.
c.800: Celtic culture established along the Rhine.
c.200: Germanic tribes from northern Europe spread southwards.
56: Roman troops occupied camps along the Rhine.

AD
451: Invasion of the Huns.
486: Final defeat and retreat of the Romans.
c.500: Tribes from the east, such as the Vandals, Burgundians and Alemanni, settled on the Rhine.

RIVER FRONTIER

THROUGHOUT HISTORY, THE RHINE HAS PROVED A SERIOUS OBSTACLE
TO ARMIES SEEKING TO INVADE COUNTRIES ON EITHER SIDE.

THE RHINE'S FERTILE VALLEY and its convenience for transport have made it a target for many attacks throughout history. From the time of the Romans until the twentieth century, the Rhine was often a battleground. Until about 200 years ago, when the river's course was straightened and its banks raised, the Rhine was up to four kilometres wide in places. It moved slowly across its broad plain, creating large areas of marsh. Until the nineteenth century, there were no permanent bridges. Invading armies crossing slowly by boat were open to attack.

RHINELAND TUG OF WAR

By 1600, there was a clear division between France, on the west bank of the Rhine, and the collection of small German states on the east. For almost 200 years after that, the Rhine was the front line in a series of wars. The city of Mannheim, for example, was attacked several times before being captured by French troops in 1688 and burned. The city was rebuilt, only to be almost destroyed again by Austrian troops in 1795.

ALSACE AND LORRAINE

The provinces of Alsace and Lorraine, now part of France, lie between the west bank of the Rhine and the Vosges and Ardennes mountains. They were a focus for conflict between France and Germany for three centuries. Alsace and Lorraine were once German states, but France took over Alsace in 1648 and Lorraine in 1790. France and

Germany went to war again in 1870. Germany won, and took back the two provinces. When the First World War ended in 1918, Alsace and Lorraine once more became part of France – only to be invaded again by German troops in 1940. Finally, the two provinces were returned to France when Germany was defeated at the end of the Second World War in 1945.

▼ *Hardenburg Castle, near Mannheim, was burned to the ground by French soldiers in 1794 when its walls, which were seven metres thick, were too strong for the French cannon.*

LINES OF DEFENCE

Tension between France and Germany after the First World War led both countries to build strong lines of defence along the Rhine. The French fortifications were called the Maginot Line and ran from the Swiss to the Belgian border. The Germans' Siegfried Line

matched it on the east side of the Rhine. As it turned out, the lines of defence were never used. In 1940, soon after the start of the Second World War, the German army invaded France by sweeping north-west through Belgium.

CROSSING THE RHINE

In 1944, American, British and French forces, who were allies, landed in German-occupied France. Their aim was victory by the end of the year. But although they drove the German army out of France and Belgium, crossing the Rhine proved more difficult. An attempt at an airborne crossing at Arnhem in September 1944 was a disastrous failure. It was not until six months later that American troops became the first foreign soldiers to cross the Rhine since 1805.

▶ *In 1945, a United States Army tank crosses the steel and concrete 'dragon's teeth', which were the outer defences of the German Siegfried Line.*

THE BRIDGE AT REMAGEN

As German troops retreated across the Rhine in March 1945, they blew up the bridges behind them. The railway bridge at Remagen, 20 kilometres south of Bonn, was mined with explosives like the others. The fuse was lit, but nothing happened. On 7 March 1945, over 8000 American troops crossed the bridge. Ten days later, with the Americans in command of the east bank of the Rhine, the bridge collapsed.

LEGENDS OF THE RHINE

To the German people, the Rhine is *Vater Rhein*, Father Rhine, and the river is the setting for many German folk stories.

▲ The Lorelei sings in the moonlight on the rock which is today a popular tourist attraction. ▶

One of the most famous Rhine legends is the story of the Lorelei, a sheer slate rock which towers 131 metres above the river near the small town of Kaub. Until about 200 years ago, there were reefs and rapids nearby that were extremely dangerous for sailors. The Lorelei is famous for the way the wind echoes in its caves and gullies, and it was this that gave rise to its story.

LORELEI'S TRAP

A cave in the rock was the home, so the tale goes, of a beautiful maiden, Lorelei, who bewitched passing sailors with her singing. Hoping to catch sight of the singer, the sailors stared at the rock, losing their concentration, which resulted in their boats being dashed to pieces on the reefs. When the son of a nobleman was lured to his death in this way, his father sent troops to the rock with orders to hunt down and kill Lorelei. They found her cave empty and settled down to

◀ *The* Mausetürm *near Bingen where, according to the legend, Archbishop Hatto met his fate.*

THE LEGENDARY HERO SIEGFRIED

Siegfried is the hero of a collection of German legends first written down about 800 years ago. Most of Siegfried's 39 adventures took place along the Rhine. One story tells how Siegfried took charge of a huge hoard of treasure that he carried with him wherever he went. He was killed by his enemy Hagen, who loaded the treasure on to ships and sank it in the river. People from the area like to believe that the treasure is still somewhere on the bed of the river waiting to be reclaimed.

wait for her to return. On her way home, Lorelei saw them and called upon Father Rhine for help. The river rose up in great foaming waves, carrying her away, never to be seen again. But sailors used to say that sometimes, as they passed by, they heard mysterious singing from the rock.

THE KILLER MICE

Another of the Rhine's legends is about the *Mausetürm*, or Mouse Tower, on the river near Bingen. This belonged to Archbishop Hatto of Mainz, the ruler of the city, who lived from about AD 850 to 919. The story goes that he was a wickedly cruel man. His last cruel act took place when the starving poor of Mainz

came to him to plead for food. He sent them to a barn where, he told them, they would find corn. Once they were all inside, he ordered them to be locked in and the barn was set alight. But the poor were avenged by the mice, with the help of the river. The mice fled from the blazing barn. They turned on the Archbishop, who escaped across the river to the *Mausetürm*. A vast horde of mice set out in pursuit. The river slowed its current to let them swim easily across. Once on the other bank, the mice invaded the *Mausetürm* and ate the Archbishop.

It makes a good story, but it is quite untrue! The real purpose of the *Mausetürm* was to collect *maut* - the old German word for 'toll' - from passing ships. As for Archbishop Hatto, the truth is that he died peacefully in his bed.

THE UPPER RHINE

IN THE SOUTH-WESTERN CORNER OF GERMANY, TWO OF EUROPE'S MOST IMPORTANT RIVERS, THE RHINE AND THE DANUBE, PASS WITHIN ABOUT 30 KILOMETRES OF EACH OTHER, FLOWING IN OPPOSITE DIRECTIONS.

Danube
Rhine
Basle Schaffhausen Lake
Falls Constance
LIECHTENSTEIN
AUSTRIA
SWITZERLAND
Vorderrhein
Lake Toma
Hinterrhein
Rheinwaldhorn Glacier

THE DANUBE IS ON ITS WAY EASTWARDS THROUGH AUSTRIA and the Balkan Mountains to the Black Sea. The Rhine is still flowing west, forming the border between Germany and Switzerland. This is Europe's great watershed, the point from which rivers and streams flow away in different directions. It is strange to think that if, 50 million years ago, the earth's crust had settled in a slightly different pattern, Europe's geography and history would have been entirely different.

LAKE OF PLENTY

The major feature of the upper Rhine is Lake Constance, known to Germans as the *Bodensee*. It is the second largest lake in Europe, with an area of 530 square kilometres, which is about the size of the Isle of Man. At its longest point, it is 63.5 kilometres long and its greatest width is 14 kilometres. Austria, Germany and Switzerland all have their borders on its shores. Lake Constance acts as a kind of safety-valve for flood water. Water pours into it from the Rhine and from many smaller streams on its southern shore. These streams, and the Rhine itself, can become torrents in the spring and early summer when the Alpine snow melts. Lake Constance holds this surplus water and releases it more slowly downstream, although it still falls dramatically over the Schaffhausen Falls.

The lake is surrounded by fertile soil made up of deposits of rock fragments from the mountain streams. Over 5000 years ago this

▲ *The water supply from streams high in the Alps supports small, isolated farms.*

THE SCHAFFHAUSEN FALLS

Schaffhausen, at the western end of Lake Constance, is where the Rhine escapes from the Alps to make its way through western Europe. The waterfalls are 23 metres high and are Europe's biggest. They do not compare with Niagara's 49 metres, or the 128 metres of Africa's Victoria Falls, but they have attracted and excited tourists for over 200 years.

◀ *The Schaffhausen Falls*

soil attracted settlers, who built homes on stilts above the marshy land on the shores. Up to 200 years ago there were still large areas of marsh at the eastern end of the lake. In the nineteenth century it was decided to drain the marshy land so that it could be used for farming. This process is known as 'reclaiming' the land. A dam was built to check the flow of silt, and the Rhine was diverted along a new channel, leaving the deposits behind.

BASLE

The city that dominates the upper Rhine is Basle. It is the highest point on the river that can be reached by commercial barges. Basle was a Roman city, but even before that it was one of the great trading points of Europe. It was ideally placed for merchants from north, south, east and west; the Rhine flowed past and soon turned north, and it was at the meeting point of mule-tracks over the Alpine passes to Italy. Today, Basle is still a venue for trade fairs, and like many old trading cities it is a busy banking centre. But its main activity is the production of chemicals. Three giant international chemical companies have factories there.

▼ *Basle, Switzerland's second largest city, lies on the bend of the Rhine where it turns sharply northwards.*

THE RIFT VALLEY

THE RIVER FLOWS SLOWLY THROUGH A FLAT-BOTTOMED, STEEP-SIDED RIFT VALLEY THAT IS ABOUT 32 KILOMETRES WIDE. HERE THE RIVER FORMS THE BORDER BETWEEN GERMANY AND FRANCE.

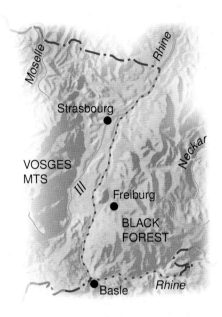

▼ *Terraced vineyards in the rift valley. Germany is the fourth largest producer of wine in the world, after France, Italy and Spain. Most of its wine comes from the valleys of the middle Rhine.*

THE RHINE'S OLD NATURAL COURSE meandered and frequently changed direction. Spring floods turned riverside land into swamp, making it useless for growing crops or raising livestock, and unhealthy for local people. In 1830, huge engineering works were carried out to straighten the Rhine, build flood banks and drain the swamps. When the scheme was finished in 1876, the course of the Rhine between Basle and Strasbourg was shorter by 82 kilometres. The width of the river, which had been up to four kilometres, was reduced to 200 metres. About 10,000 hectares of land was reclaimed for farming. The scheme was not a total success. The deepening of the river bed increased the flow of water and more silt was carried downstream. The silt was deposited and sandbanks and islands began to form along the newly-straightened river. Today, the river bed has to be dredged continuously to keep the Rhine navigable.

THE BLACK FOREST

The Black Forest covers an area of about 4500 square kilometres, which is about the size of Kent. The Rhine flows round it to the south and west. The Neckar, which joins the Rhine at Mannheim, forms the northern boundary. The Black Forest is a reminder of the time, up to about 1000 years ago, when almost all of Europe was covered with dense forests. Vast areas were cleared for farming and settlement, fuel and building material. But the Black Forest survived.

For centuries, the prosperity of the Black Forest came mainly from its timber. Today, most of the timber is sent down the Rhine as logs, either on barges or lashed together to make rafts drawn by tugs. But there are also sawmills in many of the Black Forest valleys. These provide sawn timber for small wood-based industries, which make toys, clocks, furniture and musical instruments.

Streams and rivers flow westwards through the Black Forest towards the Rhine. The warm, south-facing slopes of their valleys are ideal for growing grapes, and wine-making

▼ *Gathering grapes in the Rhine vineyards. Hand-picked grapes are used for the more expensive wines.*

has been an important industry along the Rhine for over 1000 years. Many of the slopes are terraced. They are built up to form a series of level platforms. They keep the soil moist and prevent it from being washed away, which makes cultivation of the vines easier.

◀ *A sawmill in the Black Forest. The forest's dark pines, from which it got its name, are the basis of the timber industry. Pine is renewable timber, which means that it can be harvested young and replaced with new trees.*

VISITING THE BLACK FOREST

The Black Forest attracts over two million visitors each year. Many come to enjoy walking in the forest, where there are 21,000 kilometres of long-distance footpaths. Rock-climbing, camping, mountain-biking, jogging, and winter sports are other attractions.

THE MIDDLE RHINE

As the Rhine leaves the rift valley behind, the French border swings away westwards. From now on, the Rhine has German land along both banks as far as the Netherlands' border.

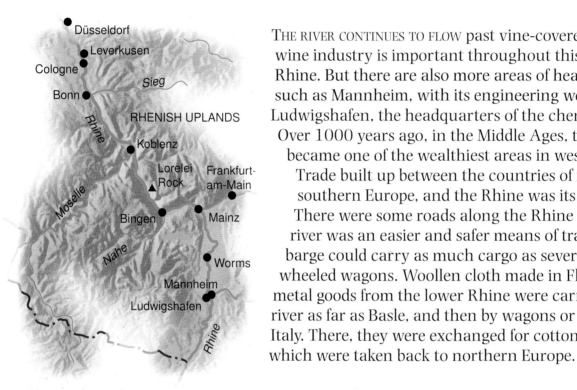

The river continues to flow past vine-covered hills, and the wine industry is important throughout this stretch of the Rhine. But there are also more areas of heavy industry such as Mannheim, with its engineering works, and Ludwigshafen, the headquarters of the chemical giant BASF. Over 1000 years ago, in the Middle Ages, the Middle Rhine became one of the wealthiest areas in western Europe. Trade built up between the countries of northern and southern Europe, and the Rhine was its main channel. There were some roads along the Rhine valley, but the river was an easier and safer means of transport. One barge could carry as much cargo as several dozen four-wheeled wagons. Woollen cloth made in Flanders and metal goods from the lower Rhine were carried south by river as far as Basle, and then by wagons or pack-horses to Italy. There, they were exchanged for cotton, silks and spices, which were taken back to northern Europe.

▼ The small town of Bacharach stands by the Rhine at the feet of the vineyards which give most of the inhabitants their living.

NOBLEMEN AND MERCHANTS

The Romans built fortresses at places along the river like Worms, Mainz and Koblenz. As trade grew, these became walled cities, which were the homes of merchants. Merchants needed the services of bankers, moneylenders and lawyers, and of craftspeople such as jewellers, goldsmiths, tailors and dressmakers. In this way, a string of prosperous cities built up along the Middle Rhine.

THE BINGEN GORGE

Near Mainz, the Rhine turns sharply to the west to find a way through the Rhenish Uplands, a group of wooded mountain ranges rising to 880 metres. When the Rhine was being formed 50 million years ago, its waters

collected at this point, unable to find an outlet. Finally, they broke through at Bingen Hole, a deep craggy-sided gorge. In the past, many Rhine sailors were swept to their deaths against the rocky sides or on hidden reefs on the river bed. In 1830, dynamite was used to clear some of the reefs and widen the river.

FLOOD DANGER

Despite all the work that has been done along the Middle Rhine since 1830, the river is still troubled by floods. Between Strasbourg and Cologne, the Rhine is fed by a number of major tributaries. The Ill joins it near Strasbourg, the Neckar at Mannheim, the Main at Mainz, the Nahe at Bingen, the Moselle at Koblenz and the Sieg at Bonn. Draining the high land of western Germany and eastern France, these tributaries carry down with them large amounts of sediment. Some of this drops to the river bed as they join the Rhine. Added to this, the Rhine's own course is almost level and slow-flowing

▼ *Despite centuries of work to prevent flooding, freak weather can still bring chaos to the cities of the Rhine. This was the scene in Cologne in 1995, following heavy storms.*

through this area and it carries its own sediment. Left untouched, these sediments would not only build up on the river banks but would also form islands in mid-river. Keeping the Rhine open for barge traffic is a major priority. Dredgers work to scoop out the sediment and prevent shallows and islands from forming. But it is not only shipping that is at risk if sediment builds up on the river bed. The climate of northern Europe is unpredictable. If storms come at the same time as the Rhine is full of water from the mountains, serious flooding is the result.

▼ *A giant dredger at work. Dredging is necessary not only to keep the river open for shipping, but also to prevent sediment building up on the river bed and causing floods.*

THE LOWER RHINE PLAIN

FOR THE LAST 350 KILOMETRES OF ITS JOURNEY TO THE NORTH SEA,
THE RHINE CROSSES AN ALMOST LEVEL PLAIN, FLOWING SLOWLY
NORTHWARDS ON A MEANDERING COURSE.

▼ *A satellite view of the Rhine in the Cologne area. Cologne is at the northern end of the eastward meander in the centre. The red areas are vegetation. Built-up areas are dark blue-grey. This type of photograph is called a 'false-colour satellite image'.*

COLOGNE STANDS AT THE southern end of the Lower Rhine Plain. It has been one of the major trading cities of Europe for over 1000 years. Today, with a population of more than one million, it is by far the largest city on the Rhine. Cologne's prosperity was based on trade. It stood at the point on the Rhine where cargoes from abroad had to be transferred from ocean-going ships to smaller river boats, which carried them inland. Old trade routes led from France to the east and from northern Germany and beyond to the west. In the nineteenth century, canals and railways followed these routes, strengthening Cologne's position as a communications centre. It is still a major port and industrial city, despite having been almost completely destroyed by bombing during the Second World War.

DYES AND CHEMICALS

This stretch of the Rhine has links with the textile industry, which goes back at least 500 years. Water is vital to the

◀ *Cologne from the air. The cathedral, top centre, was almost the only building left standing after Allied air raids in the Second World War. After the War, the city was entirely rebuilt.*

manufacture of cloth. It was once a source of power for spinning and weaving, and a constant water supply is also needed for processes such as dyeing. The town of Krefeld was a centre for spinning, weaving and dyeing by about 1500. Further south, on the outskirts of Cologne, a dye manufacturer called Carl Leverkus built a new town, which he called Leverkusen, around his factory in the nineteenth century. Today, Leverkusen is the headquarters of Bayer, one of the world's leading manufacturers of chemicals.

MEANDERS AND OX-BOWS

North of Cologne, the Rhine begins to meander in great loops. The plain is made up of soft deposits of silt brought down by the river over thousands of years. The silt does not stop the water, which undercuts the banks on the outside curves, where it flows fastest, leaving more deposits on the inside. In time, the curves become wider and wider until the river breaks through the 'neck' of the meander and the whole process begins again. The water cut off by the new channel is called an ox-bow lake. Changes in a river's course take place gradually, but they can have serious consequences for people who live nearby.

▼ *Today's chemical industry in Krefeld had its beginnings in dyes for textiles.*

MEANDERS

1. Slow-flowing river begins to form a loop.
2. The loop widens to become a meander. The outer bank of each curve is undercut.
3. Water breaks through the undercut 'neck' of the meander and finds a new course.
4. A new bank is formed, cutting off the old meander, which becomes an ox-bow lake.

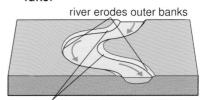
river erodes outer banks

river deposits material on inner banks
the meander develops

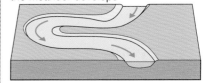

erosion causes river to cut through the narrow neck of land

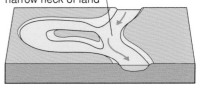

deposition causes the meander to be blocked off

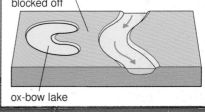
ox-bow lake

THE RUHR

THE RIVER RUHR IS A TRIBUTARY OF THE RHINE, WHICH IT JOINS AT DUISBURG. IT GAVE ITS NAME TO THE AREA THAT BECAME GERMANY'S MAIN CENTRE OF HEAVY INDUSTRY.

THE RUHR WAS A FARMING DISTRICT with a few scattered shallow coal-mines. Then, in 1841, the first deep mine was sunk, opening up thick seams of high quality coal. This was the start of the Ruhr's industrial history. Within thirty years the coal, iron and steel industries created a grim landscape of coal pitheads, foundries, blast furnaces and rolling-mills in a string of towns along the Ruhr valley. They imported iron ore and other raw materials, and exported their products, along the Rhine and Ruhr. Essen was the home of the giant Krupp steelworks. Gelsenkirchen specialised in chemicals extracted from coal. Bochum refined tin and zinc, as well as making iron and steel. Dortmund made

◀▲ *The new Opel car assembly plant at Bochum in the Ruhr. The Opel company, whose headquarters are on the Rhine at Rudesheim near Mainz, produces about a quarter of Germany's annual output of cars.*

steel railway track, mining machinery and wire ropes. Duisburg, which had been a small market town, grew quickly, absorbing the neighbouring town of Ruhrort. As well as having factories of its own, it became the port for the factories and foundries of the Ruhr. Today, it is the world's largest inland port, stretching for 30 kilometres along the Rhine.

OVERCROWDING AND POLLUTION

Millions of people flocked to the Ruhr after 1850 in search of work. Some were housed in communities specially built by coal-mining companies. Groups of flats were arranged round communal gardens where families could grow some vegetables and keep goats, chickens and pigs. These were the lucky families. Others had to crowd into whatever homes they could find. The industrial towns of the Ruhr became extremely overcrowded, with all the threats to health and family life that overcrowding brings. There was no attempt to control industrial pollution, so clouds of foul, smoky air hung over the Ruhr towns, and industrial waste was allowed to pour into the river.

CHANGES IN THE RUHR

Like other heavy industry areas in Europe, the Ruhr is less busy than it was up to fifty years ago. The switch from coal to oil and natural gas as the major energy source, and competition to the steel industry from south-east Asia, have reduced its importance. But it is still Germany's key industrial area, giving work to four million people. Some industries have been able to adapt to the new conditions. Gelsenkirchen, for example, has kept its chemical industries, but they are now based on oil instead of coal. Other towns have invested in newer industries such as electronics and computers, or turned to storing and refining oil. Others again have rebuilt their factories to make iron and steel and engineering products more efficiently, using modern methods.

> ### TWO INDUSTRIAL GIANTS
> **Alfred Krupp 1812-1887**
> At 14, he took control of a small steelworks run by his widowed mother. Krupp developed high-grade steel used for armaments and locomotive parts. In his lifetime the Krupp workforce grew from 7 to 21,000.
>
> **August Thyssen 1842-1926**
> He set up an iron foundry at Duisburg in the 1860s. Thyssen later built up a huge industrial empire in heavy engineering, electrical equipment and shipbuilding and developed the port of Duisburg to service his factories.

▼ *Alfred Krupp. His work on artillery guns earned him the nickname 'The Cannon King'.*

THE CANALS OF THE RHINE

THE RHINE IS THE SPINE OF A WATERWAY SYSTEM THAT PASSES THROUGH SIX COUNTRIES - GERMANY, FRANCE, SWITZERLAND, BELGIUM, THE NETHERLANDS AND LUXEMBOURG.

OVER THE PAST 150 YEARS, the waterway system provided by the Rhine and its tributaries has been extended by canals. The rivers have been made deeper, wider and straighter to make navigation by larger vessels easier. The Rhine system gives access to the North Sea ports for towns and cities far from the sea. The Rhine system is also linked to eastern Europe and the Black Sea by the Europa Canal (see pages 40-41).

▼*Traffic on the Rhine. Container barges can carry as many as 90 six-metre containers, keeping 90 trucks off the roads.*

▼ *The first steamships on the Rhine, about 170 years ago, were paddle steamers. They are now rare, but this one, the* Goethe, *is still at work carrying tourists.*

THE CANALS OF THE RHINE

From the banks of the Rhine, canals extend into the heart of neighbouring countries. Strasbourg is one of the key points in the system. From there, the Rhône-Rhine canal runs southwards, parallel to the Rhine, before turning west to meet the Rhône, one of France's major navigable rivers. Another canal leaves the Rhine at Strasbourg and strikes due west across the French province of Lorraine to meet the river Rhône. Further north, near Duisburg, the Dortmund-Ems canal heads north-west through the industrial Ruhr area.

RIVER AND CANAL BOATS

Transport by inland waterway is slow, but it is cheaper than by road or rail. In the past, canal boats were used mainly for bulk cargoes such as coal, bricks, grain and steel. Containers, which are large metal boxes about 20 metres

long, were introduced in the 1960s. They increased the range of cargoes carried. Containers are easily transferred between ocean-going and canal craft by cranes, and between canal craft and trucks or railway wagons.

Flat-bottomed, straight-sided barges are the most common Rhine craft. Some barges are self-propelled, with their own engines and derricks for loading and unloading. But most are 'dumb barges' without power. These are pushed or towed either by self-propelled barges or by tugs. Tugs are often seen pulling trains of dumb barges. Another method of moving barges is called 'push-tow'. Loaded dumb barges are lashed to a powerful tug, which then pushes the load along. Up to six barges can be sent up or down river in this way, under the control of a single tug crew. Although many tugs and self-propelled barges are owned by large companies, some are operated by owners who have just one craft and live on board.

Cargoes arriving at Rotterdam to be sent up the Rhine are normally unloaded from ocean-going ships and re-loaded on to barges. Modern dockside equipment can carry out this task quickly and efficiently. But new developments in shipping have made the transfer of cargoes even easier. Barge-carrying ships with their own giant gantry cranes carry on board a number of barges as well as their cargoes, picking up the barges as if they were large containers. When the ship reaches its destination, barges and cargoes can be unloaded at once and be on their way.

RHINE BARGES
A standard-sized barge, used on the Rhine and all over the waterways of western Europe including the Europa Canal, can carry 1350 tonnes of cargo. It would take 32 large articulated trucks to move a load that size. Some barges used on the lower Rhine carry up to 3000 tonnes of cargo.

THE DUTCH RHINE

NETHERLANDS

Rotterdam
Lek
Arnhem
Waal
Maas
Rhine
Duisburg
Dortmund
Essen
Krefeld
Düsseldorf

IN THE LOW-LYING LAND OF THE NETHERLANDS, THE RHINE DIVIDES INTO TWO PARTS, THE LEK AND THE WAAL.

FOR MANY THOUSANDS OF YEARS, the tides sweeping from the south-west across the Atlantic Ocean have been divided by the barrier of the British Isles. One of the tides sweeps northwards up the western coasts and then southwards down the North Sea. There it meets the other tide, which comes up the English Channel. The flow of water is suddenly brought to a halt, with the result that deposits of material have built up and formed sandbanks in the North Sea and the coastal land of the Netherlands.

▼ *A canal in the Netherlands. The windmill controls the level of water in the canal and in the cross-channels which meet it at the centre of the picture.*

THE INVADING SEA

Storms combined with high tides have often brought floods to the low-lying Netherlands. Windswept tides build up new sandbanks and change the course of the mouth of the Rhine. Until AD 839 the mouth of the Rhine was about 40 kilometres north of the present main channel. Then a hurricane in the North Sea churned up enough sand to block the channel, creating a swamp because the river water could not escape. It was not until 1807 that a new channel was cut through the sand. Lock-gates were installed to control the inflow of tidal water and the outflow of the river.

DYKES AND WINDMILLS

The present-day Netherlands is almost entirely a man-made landscape. For at least 900 years its land has been reclaimed from the delta and the sea by networks of canals with earth banks called dykes. About 1200 windmills – or wind pumps, to give them their correct name – were introduced to pump the surplus water away. The windmills of the Netherlands are still a familiar sight, but electric pumps are now the basis of the drainage system.

▲ The Afsluitdijk, one of the massive sea-walls which protect the low-lying land of the Netherlands.

THE 1953 FLOODS

The Netherlands experienced its worst floods in history in January 1953. A surge of water down the North Sea, driven by hurricane-force winds, burst without warning over the sea-walls and dykes. More than 1800 people were drowned, together with 50,000 cattle. More than 500 kilometres of dykes were damaged. Salt water contaminated the land, making it useless for growing crops or grazing animals until it had been treated with chemicals. Some of the most heavily flooded land took five years before it was producing good crops again, but grassland did recover more quickly.

FARMING

With few resources of its own, the Netherlands has always had to struggle to survive. Taking advantage of its coastline, it became a great trading nation. Its fertile land provides grazing, which is the basis of a great dairy industry. The land is also ideal for growing vegetables and flower bulbs. The North Sea and the Rhine make it easy to transport these to markets in Britain and mainland Europe. The Netherlands is one of the most intensely farmed areas in the world, with 54 per cent of the land used for farming.

▼ Small ports as well as large make a good living from the Rhine. This is Willenstad in the Netherlands.

▲ Fields of tulips ready for harvesting in the Netherlands. As well as its worldwide trade in cut flowers, the Netherlands supplies 90 per cent of the world's flowering bulbs.

THE RHINE'S SEAPORTS

THE TWO MAIN SEAPORTS OF THE NETHERLANDS ARE ROTTERDAM AND AMSTERDAM. AMSTERDAM MADE THE NETHERLANDS A GREAT TRADING NATION, BUT ROTTERDAM HAS TAKEN OVER AS THE COUNTRY'S MAJOR PORT.

ROTTERDAM IS AT THE MOUTH of the combined Lek and Waal rivers, and connects directly with the Rhine. Amsterdam, to the north, has access to the North Sea but it had no link with the Rhine until a canal was built in the nineteenth century.

In the seventeenth century Amsterdam was the centre of the Netherlands' shipping trade, and became immensely rich. At that time Rotterdam was a small fishing port.

▼ *A container ship unloads at Rotterdam. Over four million containers pass through Rotterdam each year.*

THE NEW WATERWAY

As steamships replaced sail in the nineteenth century, both the size of ships and the amount of traffic increased. In 1866 work started on the New Waterway, a deep, broad channel between the city of Rotterdam and the Hook of Holland, 35 kilometres downstream. The New Waterway, which took 24 years to complete, enabled the largest ships at that time to sail up to Rotterdam. As soon as it opened in 1890 Rotterdam began to expand rapidly.

ADAPTING TO CHANGE

Rotterdam is now the busiest port in the world in terms of the cargo it handles, over 300 million tonnes each year. Its docks, oil terminals, warehouses and harbour basins extend down the New Waterway to the sea. A new extension, Europort, was opened in 1966 on the south bank of the New Waterway. Europort's quays stretch for 5 kilometres into the North Sea, and can take the largest bulk carriers and tankers. The entire Rotterdam complex has over four times as much navigable water than 50 years ago.

This growth has come about because Rotterdam has adapted to the great changes in the shipping industry over the past 50 years. The size of tankers bringing oil to Europe from the Middle East, and bulk carriers with cargoes such as coal or grain, has steadily grown. Many are too large for normal docks to handle, and this was the reason for building Europort. Rotterdam is mainland Europe's primary oil port. Over one-third of its 1992 trade was in oil, far ahead of any other port in the world.

Another great change is in the use of containers for general cargoes. Container ships need special dockside equipment to unload them and sort the containers for distribution. Ships' time in port is 'dead time', when they are not earning money, so a fast

▲ Utrecht was an important port on the Rhine until a violent storm in 1674 changed the river's course. It is still linked to the Rhine by canals, now used as leisure facilities.

THE PORT OF ROTTERDAM	
Cargo handled 1995: 305.2 million tonnes.	
Crude oil: 104.8 million tonnes.	
Refined oil: 22.5 million tonnes.	
Iron ore: 30.9 million tonnes.	
Coal: 23.8 million tonnes.	
Number of ships docked annually: 31,000	
Area of docks 1850:	39 hectares
1902:	120 hectares
1945:	500 hectares
1996:	2148 hectares

turn-round time of two to three days in port is vital. In 1992, well over four million containers passed through Rotterdam, making it the largest container port in Europe and the third in the world. Containers can travel on from Rotterdam by road or rail, or by barge up the Rhine.

TOURISTS ON THE RHINE

MOUNTAINS AND FORESTS, 'FAIRY-TALE' CASTLES, ACTIVE SPORTS AND LEISURELY RIVER CRUISES ALL ATTRACT MILLIONS OF TOURISTS.

AMONG VISITORS FROM ABROAD, people from the Netherlands make up the largest number, followed closely by tourists from the United States and then the United Kingdom. Since the destruction of the Berlin Wall and the opening up of eastern Europe in 1989, millions of visitors from the east have been able to explore the German Alps, the Black Forest and the Rhine valley for the first time.

HISTORICAL TRAVELLERS

Foreign visitors have been travelling along the Rhine since the Middle Ages, when Christian pilgrims from northern Europe made their way down the valley on their way to Rome.

Tourism in the modern sense began about 200 years ago. It became the fashion for rich young men, and some young women, to travel south to Italy. One of their favourite routes was up the Rhine by boat and over the Alpine passes by donkey.

Then, in the nineteenth century, doctors began to recommend bathing in the salt springs of towns like Bad Durkheim and Baden-Baden, high in the Black Forest, as a cure for rheumatism and other health problems. Soon, the royal and noble families of Europe were flocking to the spa towns. Many spas are still open, but today's visitors are more likely to be looking for bed-and-breakfast or a camp site than for salt baths.

◀ *Local residents as well as tourists take advantage of the banks of the lower Rhine for swimming and watersports.*

CRUISING ON THE RHINE

Many of the Rhine's most beautiful scenery is best seen from the river. Lake Constance is criss-crossed with ferry services provided by a fleet of 40 ships. Along the Rhine from Basle to Rotterdam, a variety of large and small ships provide river trips, including a five-day cruise along the whole course.

MODERN TOURISTS

The importance of tourism to the prosperity of countries along the Rhine is shown by the amount of money they have invested in attractions and services. In Switzerland, Liechtenstein and Austria, mountain chair-lifts and cable cars carry sightseers in summer and skiers in winter. Nature trails in the Black Forest attract enthusiasts for open-air activities. The towns and cities along the German Rhine offer museums, arts festivals, firework displays, holiday parks and other attractions. The German tourist industry emphasises the quality of local food and wine. Family holidays have been encouraged with the building of theme and adventure parks such as the Taunus-Wunderland near the old spa town of Wiesbaden.

FESTIVAL TIME

One custom that unites all the Rhine communities is carnival or, as it is called in the south, *Fastnacht*. This takes place along the lower Rhine on the Monday before the beginning of the Christian season of Lent. Towns and villages on the upper Rhine have their *Fastnacht* the next day, on Shrove Tuesday. Fancy dress, masks, decorated floats and marches led by town bands are all part of the celebrations. But the people of the Rhine need no excuse for a festival at any time, and many others take place through the summer and autumn.

▲ *Celebrating the wine harvest at Oberwesel. Each district has its own customs, but a procession of decorated floats and the crowning of a Wine Queen often start the festival off.*

◀ *Traditional folk-dancing, with the dancers dressed in regional costume, at a festival in Heidelberg on the River Neckar.*

HABITATS

HUMAN SETTLEMENT AND ACTIVITY ALONG THE RHINE HAVE SERIOUSLY DAMAGED ITS ANIMAL AND PLANT WILDLIFE.

ALONG THE UPPER RHINE, the greatest changes took place in the nineteenth century. When the Rhine's course was straightened and its banks raised, the increased flow of water lowered the river bed. The riverside woodlands and meadows dried out. Many species of plant and animal life, which depended on the annual flooding of the riverside land, were lost from these areas.

MEADOWS AND WOODLANDS

Since the early 1980s, as part of the international scheme to restore the natural life of the Rhine, some riverside woodlands and meadows have been restored. Plants that had almost died out, such as yellow flag iris and black bryony, flourish again. Flowering plants in turn encourage the return of fauna, from butterflies and beetles to birds. In the *Taubergieben* nature reserve near Freiburg on the eastern edge of the Rhine valley, almost 120 species of bird, including such rarities as the kingfisher and winter visitors like the cormorant, have been recorded. *Taubergieben* is one of several reserves where the original riverside environment has been either preserved or re-created. The aim is that these reserves will act as 'wildlife stepping-stones' – more natural habitats will be created from them.

▲ *The yellow flag iris flourishes in the shallows of the restored meadowland of the* Taubergieben *nature reserve. This protected environment is also a haven for kingfishers, once common along the Rhine but now rare.* ▶

▶ *The densely-wooded lower slopes of the Black Forest provide secure habitats for rare wildlife.*

NATURE RESERVES ON THE RHINE

Fubach, Lake Constance: Swamplands with over 500 species of nesting birds.

Gernsheim, the Kuhkopf Nature Reserve: A meander now cut off from the Rhine which is a habitat for many rare species of water fowl.

Freiburg, the Taubergieben Nature Reserve: Restored meadowland.

Mannheim Reibinsel: Restored meadowland.

UNDOING THE DAMAGE

It was in the 1960s that scientists realised the extent of the damage that had been done to the Rhine by pollution. They found that only about ten per cent remained of the 700–800 plant and animal species that used to live in the Rhine. Of fifty fish species, only twelve were left.

After the Sandoz disaster in 1986 (see page 39), the Rhine countries agreed on the Rhine Action Programme. The aim was to improve water quality so that fish like salmon and sea trout – among the species most sensitive to pollution – would return to the river. Dykes were opened or lowered to restore the flood plains. In other places, new waterways were opened up running alongside the Rhine. The flow of water was carefully controlled to encourage the settlement of fish, birds, plants and insect species that had deserted the faster mainstream.

RE-STOCKING THE BLACK FOREST

In the Black Forest, the main problem is the large area of conifers destroyed by the effects of acid rain. In some areas, large quantities of chalk have been used in an attempt to neutralise the acidity of the soil. Another hopeful move is the setting-up of a 'seed bank'. Selected tree seeds are being collected and stored until it is safe to plant them without them being damaged.

On the lower slopes of the forest, where the trees are deciduous, the balance of nature has been less damaged. They are still the homes of the European wildcat, pinemartens, black woodpeckers, black grouse and other rare species. Here, the main problem is the population explosion of deer, which is being controlled to avoid tree damage.

THE POISONED RIVER

WATER FROM THE GLACIERS OF THE ALPS STARTS ITS JOURNEY DOWN THE RHINE AS PURE AS ANY WATER COULD BE. BY THE TIME IT ARRIVES AT THE MOUTH OF THE RIVER, IT CONTAINS THOUSANDS OF DIFFERENT CHEMICALS.

HOW DID THE RHINE COME TO BE IN THIS STATE? It happened without anyone noticing. Over the past 150 years, industries of all kinds have grown up along the river. It was convenient to bring raw materials along the Rhine and to use it to carry away finished goods. Water for industrial processes could be taken from the river. More dangerously, the river was used to carry away wastes contaminated with chemicals used in industry. Today, pollution of the Rhine begins with the giant chemical factories of Basle and continues all the way to the sea. Even processes that seem 'clean', like papermaking, produce wastes from the chemicals used to bleach or colour paper. Pollution does not only affect the river water. Much of it pours out into the North Sea, where it can poison marine life.

GUILTY FARMERS

Industry is not the only culprit. Along the Rhine, and in the valleys whose rivers flow into it, farmers use huge amounts of chemical fertilisers and pesticides to improve their crops. These chemicals eventually seep into the ground. They find their way into underground streams and so into the rivers. Household wastes, too, flow into the Rhine. There is also pollution from the wastes of the nine nuclear power stations along the river, and discharges of oil from barges.

▼ *The BASF chemical works beside the Rhine at Ludwigshafen. One fifth of the world's production of chemicals comes from factories along the Rhine.*

CLEANING UP

By 1970 it was said that the Rhine was a 'dead river'. Its water was so lacking in oxygen that it could not support any form of animal life for much longer. Governments of the Rhine countries agreed on a clean-up programme. Household and industrial wastewater had to be treated before it was released into the river. Within a few years, pollution had been cut in some parts of the river by 90 per cent. Some species of fish returned to parts of the river where they had not been seen for many years. Then disaster struck.

THE SANDOZ SPILLAGE

In November 1986, fire broke out at the Sandoz chemical works in Basle. Thirty tonnes of mercury and other poisons leaked into the Rhine. Within a week, half a million fish had died and the effects had spread downstream to the North Sea. The international effort to clean up the Rhine had to start all over again.

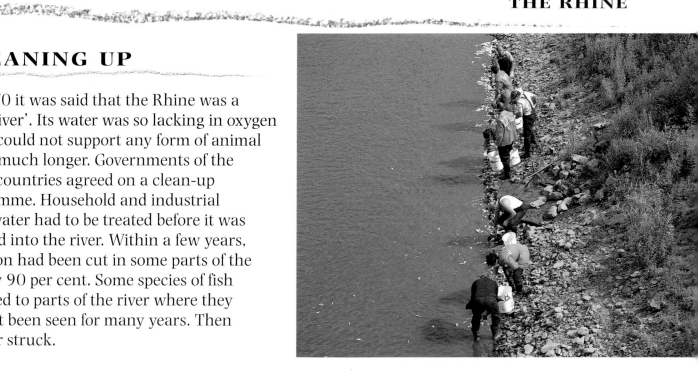

▲ Collecting dead fish from the Rhine after the Sandoz disaster in 1986. Meanwhile, below the surface, divers were pumping millions of tonnes of poisoned mud from the river bed.

ACID RAIN

Pollution in the air is also a threat to wildlife. Early in the 1970s, trees in the Black Forest began to die mysteriously. By 1985 over half the trees had died or were badly damaged. Tests showed that the soil had become more acid. It had been polluted by 'acid rain'. A major cause of acid rain is poisonous fumes from factory and power station chimneys far away. Most countries have now agreed to target dates for removing the poisons before they can be released into the atmosphere.

◀ Acid rain damage to conifers in the Black Forest. Oxides of sulphur and nitrogen carried in rainclouds are deposited and seep into the soil, changing its chemistry and attacking tree roots.

THE EUROPA CANAL

IN 1992, AN IDEA THAT HAD BEEN IN THE MINDS OF EUROPEANS FOR
1200 YEARS BECAME A REALITY. THE EUROPA CANAL, LINKING THE
RHINE, THE MAIN AND THE DANUBE, WAS OPENED.

THE COMBINED CANAL and river route takes barges through the heart of Europe on a journey of 3500 kilometres.

CHARLEMAGNE'S CANAL

The idea of a waterway crossing Europe from the North Sea to the Black Sea is over 1200 years old. In south-eastern Germany the upper waters of the Main and the Altmuhl, a tributary of the Danube, are only about 15 kilometres apart. The first attempt to link the rivers was made in the eighth century by the great Emperor Charlemagne, who ruled over

◀ In the 8th century Emperor Charlemagne ordered work to start on a canal linking eastern and western Europe.

▼ The Europa Canal winds its way towards the Swabian Alps.

most of north-western Europe. His canal was never finished, but the remains of it can still be seen.

The next scheme began in 1837 when the Ludwig Canal was cut. This made a link 161 kilometres long between Bamberg on the Regnitz, a tributary of the Main, and Dietfurt on the Altmuhl. But the canal was limited to very small barges, and it was not a success.

THE NEW PLAN

Work began in 1960 to cut a new canal between Bamberg and Kelheim, on the Danube itself. By 1970 the new canal, starting from Bamberg, had reached Nuremberg, 70 kilometres away. It took another twelve years to continue the link to Kelheim.

South of Nuremberg are the Swabian Alps, a range of hills on the north bank of the Danube. Crossing this barrier was the biggest problem for the engineers planning the canal. They solved it by building a series of locks that carry barges in steps over the range, reaching a height of over 400 metres. Each lock is 190 metres long and 12 metres wide.

The Swabian Alps were not the only obstacle. On the borders of Romania and Serbia, near the town of Orsova, the Danube broadens out and then suddenly plunges into

a gorge over a series of rapids called the Iron Gates. These were by-passed by a canal in the 1890s, but it was too narrow for modern barges. It was replaced by a new canal with two locks that can take larger vessels. Close to the Black Sea in Romania, below the industrial city of Galati, the Danube divides into three and crosses a marshy delta. In 1984, as part of the Europa scheme, a canal was built about 160 kilometres upstream between the Danube and Romania's main port, Constanta.

The Europa Canal has already led to the growth of several important ports deep inside Europe, and helped new industries to prosper.

THE EUROPA CANAL

Length: 3500 km
Route: Rotterdam to Bamberg
(Rhine/Main) 885 km
Bamberg to Kelheim (canal) 170 km
Kelheim to Cernavoda (Danube) 2285 km
Cernavoda to Constanta (canal) 160 km
Passes through: The Netherlands, Germany, Austria, Hungary, Romania.
Borders on: Czech Republic, Slovakia, Serbia, Bulgaria.

▶ *The first boat through one of the newly-finished locks at Berching.*

THE FUTURE OF THE RHINE

IN ITS HISTORY THE RHINE HAS SEEN MANY CHANGES. NOW, MORE CHANGES ARE TAKING PLACE.

FOR CENTURIES, THE RHINE was one of Europe's major battlegrounds. With the creation of the European Community and the end of East-West tension in Europe, the danger of war is in the past. For the first time in history, French and German people on each side of the Rhine are at ease with each other and threatened by no one.

CLEANING UP

The Industrial Revolution brought grime and pollution to the Rhine. The decline in heavy industries in the Ruhr, together with greater care by those that remain, have resulted in less pollution in at least one section of the river. New industries that are replacing the old

◀ *Continuous checks on the quality of river water are part of the Rhine Action Programme. This monitoring station near Lauterbourg collects samples of water and tests them.*

▼ *Waste water once allowed to flow directly into the Rhine now passes through treatment plants like this one near Ludwigshafen.*

ones, such as electronics, telecommunications and car assembly, are 'greener'. Meanwhile, the Rhine Action Programme promises a cleaner river. But the Sandoz disaster was a grim warning, and a reminder that one fifth of the world's chemical industries are along the banks of the Rhine.

LOOKING EAST

The Europa Canal, designed to carry 50 million tonnes of cargoes each year, will certainly bring changes to the lower Rhine. For centuries, the attention of Rhineland trade and business has been focused north-westwards, towards the Rhine's outlet in the North Sea. The Europa Canal provides a new link with south-eastern Europe and beyond. It is too early yet to say what effect this will have on the pattern of economic life along the Rhine. It will make it easier for Rhine products to find new markets, but it will also open up north-western Europe to products from the south-east.

THE LIVING RIVER

The most important changes in the Rhine have taken place over the past 200 years and have been made by human activity. Without this, the Rhine valley would by now be one vast flood plain and the river mouth in the North Sea would have moved many times. Human settlement brings change. But people are more aware today than they were in the past that human interference can sometimes have unexpected and damaging consequences. When there was war between France and Germany, keeping a watch on the Rhine meant keeping a lookout for the enemy. Today, it means taking care to do no further harm to one of Europe's major sources of life.

▲ *The opening of the Europa Canal could bring new opportunities and new challenges to older Rhineland cities like Strasbourg.*

◄ *The Rhine now flows between countries united in the European Community.*

GLOSSARY

armaments weapons of war

bulk carrier a ship that carries loose cargoes such as coal or grain

container a metal box of a standard size used to transport goods by sea, road or rail

course the journey that a river makes from its source to its mouth

crust the outer layer of the Earth's surface

current the flow of water in a channel

delta the area of flat land, made up of silt, at the mouth of a river

derrick a crane fixed in position on a dockside or on a ship's deck to load and unload cargo

downstream further down a river towards its mouth

dredge to clear loose material from the bed of a river or the sea to make a deep channel for ships

dumb barge barge without an engine that needs to be towed

dyke a bank built beside the sea or a river to prevent flooding

false-colour satellite image a photograph taken from space that uses unnatural colours to highlight certain features

fault a crack in the Earth's crust

foundry a factory where iron or steel is made

gantry an overhead frame with tracks supporting a crane

geologist a scientist who studies rocks

glacier a moving sheet of thick ice

harbour basin the land round a harbour containing docks and quays

hurricane a fierce storm with winds strong enough to uproot trees and damage buildings

meander winding S-shaped bends of a river

mouth the point where a river meets the sea

navigable wide and deep enough to be used by ships and boats

ox-bow lake a lake formed when a river cuts through a meander to make a new course

pithead the machinery on the surface of a coal-mine

reclaimed land land once covered by water that has been drained to allow people to farm it or build on it

rift valley a valley formed by the sinking of land between two cracks, or faults, in the Earth's crust

screes patches of loose rock and stones

sediment ground-down pieces of rock and other material carried along by a river and later deposited on the river banks and bed

silt mud and sand deposited at the mouth of a river

source the place where a river starts its journey to the sea

terraced slopes hillsides that have been cultivated so that they form a series of stepped, flat surfaces

tributary a smaller river that flows into a large river

upstream higher up a river towards its source

INDEX